Drawing Fun

HOW TO DRAW Horses

by Kathryn Clay

illustrated by June Brigman

Capstone press

Mankato, Minnesota

Snap Books are published by Capstone Press,
151 Good Counsel Drive, P.O. Box 669, Mankato, Minnesota 56002.
www.capstonepress.com

Library of Congress Cataloging-in-Publication Data

Clay, Kathryn.
    How to draw horses / by Kathryn Clay; illustrated by June Brigman.
    p. cm. — (Snap books. Drawing fun)
    Includes bibliographical references and index.
    Summary: "Lively text and fun illustrations describe how to draw horses" — Provided by publisher.
    ISBN-13: 978-1-4296-2306-3 (hardcover)
    ISBN-10: 1-4296-2306-3 (hardcover)
    1. Horses in art — Juvenile literature. 2. Drawing — Technique — Juvenile literature. I. Brigman, June. II. Title.
III. Series.
NC783.8.H65C58 2009   2008033227
743.6'96655 — dc22

Credits
Juliette Peters, designer
Abbey Fitzgerald, colorist

Photo Credits
Capstone Press/TJ Thoraldson Digital Photography, 4 (pencil), 5 (all), 32 (pencil)

The author dedicates this book to her parents, Gary and Norma.

1 2 3 4 5 6 14 13 12 11 10 09

Table of Contents

Getting Started..........................4
Must-Have Materials.............5

Head Study 6
Clydesdale...........................8
Foal 10
Grazing Horse.....................12
Horse Resting 14
Braided Beauty....................16
Bucking Bronco...................18
Dancing Lipizzan................20
Racing Arabian...................22
Appaloosa 24
Thoroughbred and Rider..26

Glossary 30
Read More 31
Internet Sites 31
Index....................................32

Getting Started

You're a budding artist who doodles on every piece of paper you find. You see a world filled with objects waiting to be sketched. You're never without a notepad and a pencil. With your talent and these step-by-step instructions, your scribbles will soon become "mane" attractions.

Maybe you want to draw elegant show horses? Practice drawing the dancing Lipizzan. Would you rather work on exciting action shots? Try sketching the Arabian as it sprints through falling leaves. Are you really into racehorses? Then check out the Thoroughbred and rider.

Of course, horses have many unique styles and traits. Once you've mastered some of the horses in this book, you'll be able to draw your own elegant equines. Let your creative side loose, and see what kinds of horses you can create.

Must-Have Materials

1. First you'll need something to draw on. Any blank, white paper will work well.

2. Pencils are a must for these drawing projects. Be sure to keep a bunch nearby.

3. Because sharp pencils make clean lines, you'll be sharpening those pencils a lot. Have a pencil sharpener handy.

4. Even the best artist needs to erase a line now and then. Pencil erasers wear out fast. A rubber or kneaded eraser will last much longer.

5. To make your drawings pop off the page, use colored pencils or markers.

Head Study

The head is the most important — and most difficult — part of drawing a horse. Give this horse a long muzzle and two alert ears. Then add an eye, nostril, mouth, and mane.

Once you've mastered the head, try drawing the rest of the horse's body.

STEP 1

STEP 2

STEP 3

STEP 4

Clydesdale

Clydesdales have bodies that are larger and thicker than other horses. But even though they look big and tough, these horses are actually very gentle. Draw this horse with a short tail. Cover the legs and hooves with long, white hair called feather.

After drawing one Clydesdale, draw a team of horses pulling a sleigh through deep snow.

STEP 1

STEP 2

STEP 4

STEP 3

Foal

Foals can walk right after birth and are able to gallop within a few hours. Their legs are almost as long as an adult horse's, but their hooves are much smaller. It almost looks like they're walking on tiptoe.

After drawing this foal, try drawing its mother standing nearby.

STEP 1

STEP 2

STEP 3

STEP 4

Grazing Horse

Horses have small stomachs, so they can't eat a lot at once. Instead, they eat many small meals throughout the day. Draw this horse nibbling on some thick grass.

Try drawing this horse munching on other favorite snacks like apples, carrots, or sugar cubes.

STEP 1

STEP 2

STEP 3

STEP 4

Horse Resting

Horses lie down for just a short time each day. That's because they can sleep standing up. And unlike humans, horses only need a few hours of sleep each day. For this horse to be comfortable, draw the front legs bent underneath and the hind legs stretched out.

Horses feel safer when they rest in groups. Draw several horses lying down near one another.

STEP 1

STEP 2

STEP 3

STEP 4

Braided Beauty

Horse manes and tails were first braided to prevent them from getting pulled out while the horses worked. Now it's all about showing off at a horse show and impressing the judges. Get this horse ready for its big debut with a beautifully braided mane and tail.

Once you've mastered the braids, add some colorful flowers to create a show-stopping style.

STEP 1

STEP 2

Bucking Bronco

You wouldn't want to take this wild bronco for a casual ride. Instead this horse is ready to entertain large crowds at a rodeo. Draw this energetic equine with two legs kicking up dirt.

After drawing this horse, draw a brave rodeo cowboy taking a wild ride.

STEP 1

STEP 2

STEP 3

STEP 4

Dancing Lipizzan

Lipizzans are shorter than most horses, but they're very strong. Their muscular legs help them perform incredible jumps and stunts to amaze audiences. Draw this horse balancing on its hind legs to perform a pirouette.

Once you've mastered this drawing, draw the horse leaping through the air.

STEP 1

STEP 2

STEP 3

STEP 4

Racing Arabian

Arabians are a popular breed because of their speed and endurance. Their deep chests and large nostrils allow them to run for miles. Check out this horse's mane and tail blowing wildly in the wind as she runs through falling leaves.

After drawing this horse, draw a group of Arabians racing through a field.

STEP 1

STEP 2

STEP 3

STEP 4

Appaloosa

Appaloosas are known for their spotted coats and their calm, cooperative personalities. Their relaxed behavior makes them perfect horses for beginning riders. To get this horse ready for a rider, add a saddle blanket, saddle, and bridle.

Once you've drawn the saddle, draw a rider ready to take the reins.

STEP 1

STEP 2

STEP 3

STEP 4

Thoroughbred and Rider

Thoroughbreds make great racehorses because of their speed. In fact, they're the fastest of all horse breeds. This horse and rider are competing in a show jumping competition. In this type of event, a rider takes the horse through tall jumps.

After mastering this drawing, draw the horse and rider racing toward the final jump.

STEP 1

STEP 2

STEP 3

STEP 4

STEP 5

To finish this drawing, turn to the next page. ⇨

STEP 6

STEP 7

STEP 8

breed (BREED) — a particular type of horse

bridle (BRYE-duhl) — the straps that fit around a horse's head and connect to a bit to control a horse while riding

bronco (BRAHNG-ko) — a wild horse

endurance (en-DUR-enss) — the ability to keep doing an activity for long periods of time

equine (i-KWINE) — a member of the horse family

foal (FOHL) — a horse that is less than 1 year old

muzzle (MUHZ-uhl) — an animal's nose, mouth, and jaws

pirouette (peer-OOH-et) — a move in which the horse stands up on its hind legs and turns in a circle

Read More

Hanson, Anders. *Cool Drawing: The Art of Creativity for Kids*. Cool Art. Edina, Minn.: Abdo, 2009.

Levin, Freddie. *1-2-3 Draw Horses: A Step-By-Step Guide*. 1-2-3 Draw. Columbus, Ohio: Peel Productions, 2004.

Perard, Victor. *You Can Draw Horses*. Mineola, N.Y.: Dover, 2006.

Smith, Lucy. *The Usborne Book of Horses and Ponies*. New York: Scholastic, 2006.

Internet Sites

FactHound offers a safe, fun way to find educator-approved Internet sites related to this book.

Here's what you do:

1. Visit *www.facthound.com*
2. Choose your grade level.
3. Begin your search.

This book's ID number is 9781429623063.

FactHound will fetch the best sites for you!

Index

Appaloosas, 24
Arabians, 4, 22

body
    heads, 6
    legs, 8, 10, 14, 18, 20
    manes, 6, 16, 22
    nostrils, 6, 22
    stomachs, 12
    tails, 8, 16, 22
broncos, 18

Clydesdales, 8

drawing supplies, 5

foals, 10

horses
    and braiding, 16
    and competitions, 16, 26
    eating, 12
    jumping, 20, 26
    racing, 22, 26
    resting, 14

Lipizzans, 4, 20

rodeos, 18

saddles, 24

Thoroughbreds, 4, 26